LOOKING OVER THE FENCE

ESSAYS BY MARION BAILEY

To Sue,

Love,

Marion

© Marion Bailey, 2016. All rights reserved, with the exception of the passage quoted from Elizabeth Bishop's poem, "One Art."

Tenth editon, February, 2016

INTRODUCTION

COMMUNITY
Property Lines I.. 11
Property Lines II... 15
The Handyman.. 17
Breakup... 21
Gone to the Dogs... 23
Bad Hair Days... 25
Afternoons at the Opera..................................... 29
Hotels... 31

FAMILY
N.M.. 39
Hawk Family... 43
Country Life... 49
City Life... 53
Beaches... 57

FRIENDS
Visiting Alice.. 63
Heath.. 69
The Salvation Army... 73
Unlikely Friends.. 75
The Art of Losing.. 77

ACKNOWLEDGEMENTS

Introduction

Retirement scared me. I have never understood retirement parties where the guests celebrate the end of the working life of the retiree. I always loved teaching which had taken up so much of my time and energy that retirement felt like falling off a trapeze without a net. But after forty years in the classroom, first in a high school in New York City and then in a community college in Massachusetts, I could barely grade my last set of essays.

The spring I retired, I arrived early for my final faculty meeting. I waited in the car for a few minutes, passing the time reading a brochure from the Beverly Senior Center. There was a small notice about a writing group that was forming.

Even though I had taught writing for many years at the community college and had taken one evening course in writing, apart from this course, I had never written anything but occasional letters and emails. I joined the group at the senior center and stayed for a year. I discovered that my fellow seniors liked what I wrote and that I liked to write. I met Liz Moon in the writing group and we decided to form a group of two, meet at the Panera Coffee Shop, exchange our writing and help one another. I would not have completed the essays here if it were not for Liz's help and encouragement.

The first group of essays is about my neighborhood which luckily for me provided a wealth of material, the second group is about my family, and the last group is about friends and colleagues.

Community

Property Lines I

Our neighbors on the corner are not speaking. A new neighbor moved in across the street and within a year our next-door neighbor, Karen, was not speaking to him. Six months later we stopped speaking to him. Three generations of Karen's family owned the land that her house is built on. Karen's grandfather gave her parents part of his land when they married, and they built the small ranch where she lives today. Next door her aunt lives in what was once the grandparents' house. The family has been protecting and defending their land for over one hundred years. When Karen's grandfather first bought the land, the next-door neighbor (where we live now) objected to Italians moving next door, so she put up a fence between the two properties. Then Karen's grandfather built a bocce court on his side of the fence, invited friends and relatives over to play, encouraged them to cheer and laugh as loudly as possible. Our next-door neighbor, who never married, lives alone now that both her parents have died. Thirty-five years ago in order to make her yard more private, Karen's mother planted fourteen fir trees on the border between Karen's house and the new neighbor.

The "new" neighbor claims the trees are on his property. Soon after they moved in, he and his wife started breaking off tree limbs. My neighbor hired a tree company to trim the trees and clean up the limbs. When Karen told the new neighbor that the tree company was coming to properly trim the trees, he called the company, telling them to stay home because the trees were his, and he planned to cut them down. Karen asked me to watch the trees when she wasn't home because she was sure the neighbor was getting ready with his chainsaw to cut down the trees when she was away. I spent a considerable amount of time at my dining room window watching the trees, after I assured her that I'd call the police if I saw him touch one.

Property Lines

Karen is sure that the trees are on her property; she knows her mother would not have planted fourteen trees on someone else's land. But because she is a careful person who loves the trees, she hired a surveyor and to be extra careful, she hired the surveyor's brother, a lawyer. Then the new neighbor hired a surveyor, but unfortunately each neighbor used the same surveyor. When he measured my neighbor's property from her side, the trees were on her property: when he measured from the new neighbor's side, the trees were on his property. Karen then called a second surveyor who measured from stakes her brother remembered her grandfather putting in the ground to mark the property — he found the trees were on her side except for the trees whose trunks had filled out — they are on the property line.

To add to the tension, the new neighbor and his brother have been riding their Harley motorcycles down our street, over my neighbor's property, through the trees and into their backyard. When Karen saw the brother racing his bike down the street, she shouted that he was on private property. He yelled obscenities at her. Luckily, Karen's cousin is a policeman who was on duty: he came over and threatened the brother with arrest. This same scenario occurred a second time, but this time the policeman (not a relative) was huge and appropriately overbearing and didn't take Karen's distress seriously. The stakes are up from both surveyors' calculations; the trees are still in place — no one is riding a motorcycle down the street but no one is talking.

That was last week. This week the neighbors with their seconds — Karen's brother, her niece and the niece's husband, his brother (big), his friend (bigger) on the new neighbor's side — were on either side of the trees, shouting across from one another, like a scene from a Quentin Tarantino movie, hatred and rage in the air. The standoff at the trees was precipitated by a letter sent from Karen's lawyer to the new neighbor stating that the trees were on her property. After he received the letter, the neighbor, his brother and a friend again started breaking off limbs from the trees. Karen told her brother, her niece and nephew to come over and the yelling started. It was an impasse — no way out of this dispute. After about ten minutes the shouting stopped. Karen called me later to say she and the neighbor were still not talking.

The dispute spilled over to our property. The day before I was leaving for Europe, I was greeted in my driveway by my next-door neighbor. She walked me over to the line between my property and the new neighbor's and said "Look what he's doing to your tree." I saw the neighbor's brother, a chainsaw in hand, cutting down a small tree on my property. According to Karen, these trees and bushes have been in this spot for fifty years. When I asked him what he was doing, he pointed to the trees and bushes separating our properties and said, "These will all be cut down by three o'clock today because that's what my brother wants." When the policeman I called arrived at my house, he tried to persuade the brother to stop. Finally, the brother agreed to stop cutting for a day — one tree was already sawdust.

Since I was leaving for two weeks, I was afraid of returning home to find all the trees and bushes gone. On that same day I was able to find a surveyor who agreed to survey the boundary line for six hundred dollars while I was away. Thanks to a recommendation from Karen and her lawyer, I hired a lawyer who sent the new neighbor a letter telling him to desist from anymore cutting until the boundary lines were settled. When I returned home fourteen days later, I found stakes in the ground and all trees and bushes where I had left them. The stakes showed (no surprise) that some of the trees and bushes were on my property, some were on his, and some were smack in the middle.

The other day I received a letter from my lawyer who so far has not charged me for his services. He laid out three choices:

1) Hire my lawyer to aggressively pursue the matter by joining in the litigation now going on between our two neighbors. This would cost between $5,000 and $10,000 to settle the issue of who owns the bushes.

2) Do nothing and wait to see what happens between our two neighbors.

3) Hire the lawyer to monitor the situation, but not to involve me in litigation. This would cost a minimum of $1,000, at $275 an hour.

I chose option 2 — do nothing and see what happens.

Three years after the shouting match at the OK Corral (the contested trees), our neighbors are still embroiled in what has turned out to be a lengthy, expensive law suit brought by Karen against the "new" neighbor over the question of who owns which trees. Twice they tried mediation, but unsurprisingly, were unable to reach a compromise. Last summer, maybe to be even more obnoxious, our "new" neighbor staged a "rock concert" in his back yard; no one from the neighborhood was invited. He placed about ten lawn chairs in a semi-circle facing a microphone with an amplifier. A singer blared songs over the entire neighborhood. The backyard audience, became louder and louder (drunker and drunker) until the final act when the new neighbor grabbed the microphone and shouted:

> *"No more trees,*
> *No more neighbors,*
> *No more trees,*
> *No more neighbors!"*

The next day the neighbors were in shock, feeling helpless against the assault. We held a meeting and agreed that each of us would call the police if it happened again — one phone call the night before produced no effect. Although I'm anticipating the next rock concert, his backyard has been strangely quiet: maybe his lawyer spoke to him, or he's lining up a singer for tomorrow night.

Property Lines II

The trees are finally down, but my neighbors, the "friendly" neighbor who lives next door and the "opposing" neighbor who lives across the street are still not talking. After four years of a bitter lawsuit, at least four lawyers, five surveyors (the first surveyor died of a heart attack) and countless failed attempts at mediation, my friendly neighbor Karen and the opposing neighbor came to an agreement. The fourteen contested fir trees would be removed by the opposing neighbor; Karen's part of the road at the end of our dead-end street would be declared her private property, insuring that the opposing neighbor and his family could never walk or park there again.

Before the trees came down, the opposing neighbor had several rock concerts in his backyard, asserting his right to hold the entire neighborhood hostage to his blaring music. The final concert at the end of the summer was the most memorable: it took place the night before the tree company came to saw down the trees. Our neighbor had written a song for the hired singer to croon into a microphone. I live across the street, but I could hear every word. The song went like this:

> *The trees are coming down*
> *The trees are coming down*
> *The surveyor's dead*
> *The surveyor's dead*
> *F— the neighbors*
> *F— the neighbors!*

About thirty guests danced and cheered reminding me of the early Israelites cavorting around the golden calf.

Three tree removal trucks arrived the next afternoon. The opposing neighbor and his wife gathered with about ten guests for what felt like witnessing a beheading. Beer was served. One of the guests was parked in front of my house with her mother on an oxygen tank in the passenger seat. When the trees started to come down, the driver got out of her car and began taking pictures on her cell phone. The excitement was over quickly because all fourteen trees (skinny trunks) were felled in under an hour.

The tree stumps were left behind because the opposing neighbor refused to pay for their removal. Karen returned to court to force the neighbor to remove the stumps because according to her lawyer removing the trees meant the whole tree — trunk, branches and stump. After the stumps were removed, Karen put up a six-foot high, eighty-foot wide white plastic fence to separate her property from opposing's property. At one end of the fence facing my side of the street are two black posts; a white chain and padlock hangs from one post so that if Karen wishes, she can block access to her end of the street. She assured me a chain is only a threat to an opposing neighbor; if he steps on her property, she'll put the chain across the road and lock it. When that happens, I'll be given a key to the padlock so I can unlock the chain for any friend or family member who needs to turn around on my narrow, dead-end street.

Karen confided that she has spent almost $200,000 on this dispute: paying lawyers, surveyors and installing a huge, elaborate fence — I can only imagine the cost to Opposing. My neighbors, on either side of the new fence, will never speak again.

The Handyman

I was scared the first time I saw him. Two cars were racing down the street, one close behind the other — he was driving the first, a fancy sports car — he sped into his driveway, ran out of the car and into the house. Across the street, a woman on the sidewalk started yelling at his departing back, telling the small crowd that had gathered that he had done "this" before. The second car drove away. What had my neighbor done? Who was this man living around the corner who could arouse such anger in people?

Paul lived in a beautifully restored 18th century house. Before I moved into the neighborhood, he had painstakingly restored his house, even burning off layers of old paint on the shingles by hand, using a blow torch. When I finally met him, I was surprised at how handsome he was. His almost movie-star looks contradicted the impression I had of him as someone weird. He looked in his fifties, tall and well-built. His thick, dark hair was striking. He was unmarried and lived with his widowed, elderly father in their big house. A few months after I met him, he had a job burning off the paint on a house even bigger than his own. Since the house was behind mine, I watched him for over two years from my kitchen window, burning and scraping the shingles, one by one, always alone, with big headphones on. I wondered how anyone could spend so much time alone.

About three years ago, he started doing various jobs on the house next door, occupied by an attractive, unmarried, childless couple in their late forties. I'd see his white truck parked in their driveway for the whole day. Because he spent so much time next door, I began to wonder whether he was living there, the third party in a *ménage a trois*. Often, the husband was away on business, and the handyman would still be there. How much work did the house need? I knew he did painting, carpentry, some plumbing and a little electrical work but was he on a permanent retainer for people who weren't wealthy? When the neighbors moved and put their house up for sale, Paul was still going in and out, with his headphones on and his own key.

Maybe I was missing out. Despite my uneasiness, I thought why not use the neighborhood handyman for some repairs; I wanted to be part of the club. Although he's not an electrician, I asked him to fix the broken light above my entryway. He said the light fixture needed to be painted, but he would paint it at home because he was on another job. Weeks later he returned the fixture, original to our old house, and beautifully painted. I put in a bulb, and turned on the light. Ten minutes later, he drove by, stopped and handed me a different bulb, one he said would give a softer light. A week later Paul installed a new chandelier over my dining room table.

A modest bill arrived in my mail box. I thought I had hit the jackpot — a neighbor who could do everything, was always available, would do the smallest job, did beautiful work and was reasonable. Thinking along these lines, I asked him to paint our front door. Although he was in the middle of a project next door, he came over the next day to paint and made sure to take off all the hardware on the door before he started (he told me most painters didn't bother). He left while the paint dried. An hour later, I needed to reach him because I was leaving, and he had to put the hardware back on so I could lock the door. I called his home phone, his father answered, and in a creaky, irritable voice told me our handyman was working next door. His father called him to tell him I needed him. Five minutes later Paul walked in the door in a rage. Brandishing his cell phone in my face, he yelled that I was never to call him at home again, that the home phone was not his phone, the cell phone was his phone although he never told me he had a cell phone. His rage was what I remembered from the first time I saw him, rushing away from someone who was chasing him. I didn't want to be around him.

But a year later I needed two upstairs bedrooms painted. The handyman had continued to work for my neighbors. How weird could he be? Plus I knew he would do a good job, and he was always available. Before he started painting, he hung out at my house for long periods of time, very comfortable and chatty, worlds apart from his angry self. He wanted my key, which I gave him, because he said he needed to come in and out when I wasn't home. I had the sense that maybe he was moving in, the way he did with the next door neighbors. The job took a long time, and I began to feel uneasy at night with my key in his possession. I felt guilty asking him for the key back (might he suspect I was afraid of him?) but after about five requests he returned it. The rooms were finally finished, beautifully done. He put three coats of paint on each of the walls — the job took forever, but at last I had two handsomely painted bedrooms.

Soon after Paul painted the bedrooms, we had what almost felt like a breakup. Like many breakups, I don't understand what happened. Paul built a banister for my staircase, but never completed the job which was unlike him. Most of the work was done expertly, as always, but he didn't finish the painting. He never returned or answered phone calls, and he never gave me a bill for the work that he had done.

Paul once told me he had his own contracting business with twenty people working for him. What happened to the business? Why did such a talented man work as the neighborhood handyman, frequently doing menial jobs like painting a bedroom? Did I make him angry when I asked for my key back? When I didn't want to hang out with him like my neighbor next door? He's friendly enough when I run into him, but it's not the same — he never worked for me again.

Breakup

They were the best neighbors you could imagine, interesting people, considerate to a fault. I remember when I first saw them many years ago. They had just put a bid on the house next door; they were sitting in their car, looking very pleased with themselves. What I remember most is that she was sitting on his lap. I brought over a bottle of lemoncello as a welcome gift — he was the only one living in the house at the time. He was getting it ready for her, painting rooms with her color choices, sanding floors. When he finished, she and her daughter moved in, along with his dog, her dog and their cat.

Although they were middle aged, she forty, he fifty, they acted like newlyweds. She wore an engagement ring, no wedding ring, but talked about getting married some day in a vague kind of way. A hot tub appeared in their backyard, close to our back porch but we never heard or saw them in it, but I could imagine them (naked?), gently splashing their feet, each with a glass of red wine. A few weeks later they put a fence around the side of the tub facing us so we couldn't see them. When I heard they were moving in with three animals I was afraid of the noise and disruption, but there never was any. If a dog barked, I didn't hear it.

For about seven years, the honeymoon period continued. He bought a convertible sports car: I'd see them driving, she with dark glasses and a scarf on her long frosted blond hair, looking like a Hollywood starlet, he with his muscular build, proudly at the steering wheel. I heard about ski trips to Utah, trips to California to visit wineries, eating in trendy restaurants in Boston, making me envy their sophisticated life.

About two years ago the house became quiet. There were no more romantic candlelit dinners on the patio; no more sitting around the outdoor fireplace with friends, drinking wine. No one worked on the yard except for a cursory mowing but even that stopped last summer. Her once beautiful flowers became overgrown and died. No attractive flower pots were on the stoop last summer. Our neighbors walked their dogs separately. Now it was one person, one dog around the neighborhood. I no longer saw them together; he didn't appear to be home much or when he was, the TV glowed blue from his rec room. He watched sports all year long, always by himself.

The silence next door became deafening, but the noise when it came was worse. Last summer I heard him yelling at her, in a rage. Apparently (I didn't hear her) she had asked him to mow the grass. His response was frightening. He started yelling at her, getting louder, nastier and angrier. I had a sense of foreboding — hearing him argue was like watching a truck going over a cliff in slow motion. I knew a horrible ending was coming. At the end of the summer he and a neighbor started moving furniture out of the house. No one said anything to me about what was going on, again silence.

A few weeks ago I saw a huge moving van parked in front of the house; the van was there for a week while he loaded up more of his stuff. Once I drove past the house and asked him, "What's going on?" He told me he got laid off from his engineering job and he wanted out: out of the house, the state, the relationship. He was taking half of the furniture, his clothes and belongings and moving to Utah to ski. She moved out a week later, without speaking to me. A For Sale Sign in front of the house is sinking lower and lower in the snow. Prospective buyers drift in and out. The hot tub, that symbol of good times, looks forlorn, turned on its side. The hydrangea tree carefully planted by both of them is still small but erect, a sign of hope if even for a brief time. A neighbor told me they were both good people, they just didn't like each other.

Gone to the Dogs

My neighborhood has changed. It used to belong to the residents and the people who walked and jogged along the streets. It's a good place for being outside because it's quiet, a few blocks from the beach and close to a park

Now the dogs rule. Not loose dogs — Beverly has a strict leash law with a heavy fine for any dog owner who allows their pet to run loose. No, these are dogs on leashes attached to owners — dogs who walk ahead of their owners with their heads held high, dogs who walk like they're the center of everyone's attention which they are. The dog in this dog age we're living in walks on the sidewalk with the owner trying to catch up. These dogs do not move when I walk toward them on a narrow sidewalk. I have to move to let them go by.

Then there's the dog who starts sniffing me. The owner invariably says "Oh, he just likes people." I feel obligated to respond to this sociable animal and bend down to pet him. The owner beams like he expects me to say more. So I mention the outstanding fur and ask the breed, always indecipherable to me. Now that the dogs have gotten control, this conversation might be repeated five times in a half hour walk

My neighborhood has become a beauty pageant for canines. The owners are the handlers and they are a club with their own rules, one of which is don't speak to non-dog owners, unless the dog initiates the encounter. I feel like I have to fit in and make it with the dogs in order to be accepted.

The other day my neighbor said, "I know you don't like Tiffany." I didn't know what she was talking about because I didn't feel one way or the other about Tiffany, a tiny, furry something or other. In fact I had never given Tiffany any thought at all. My neighbor said, "Well you never talk to her." Tiffany by the way struts around the neighborhood with two sweaters on, one for inside, the second on top of the first for outside. Now in the interest of being a good neighbor, first I talk to Tiffany, then I say hello to my neighbor.

I know that dogs are sometimes people's children. But what worries me is that dogs are starting to behave like children, spoiled children, and dog owners expect you to treat their dogs like adorable offspring.

Bad Hair Days

Hair is maybe the most important body part in the United States. We spend millions of dollars to straighten, curl, color, wash, condition, gel, mousse, and lacquer it. I have a friend who only washes her hair every ten days because it takes so much time to get her hair the way she wants. Somehow she manages to maintain her elaborate style while she sleeps.

The town of Beverly has more hair "salons" (even the name suggests importance) than grocery stores, bars, restaurants, or gift stores. Only nail "salons" are more common. I remember my mother, for a brief time, rolled my hair in cotton socks before I went to bed so that when I woke up in the morning, I could unroll the socks, and have an instant page boy. I can't imagine how I slept on those rolled up socks.

When I was teaching high school in Brooklyn, a teaching friend and I went to the same hairdresser and got identical haircuts, bangs and a shoulder-length bob. We also bought matching coats to go with our stylish haircuts. For my wedding I did my own hair. As a young mother I didn't spend much time thinking about hair but I did cut my daughters' hair: they had uneven bangs for years.

My hair problems started in middle age when I changed from a decent though unexciting hair dresser to someone, by reputation anyway, more stylish, further away and, of course, more expensive. A good friend had started referring to certain hair cuts as "the old lady style," while looking at me. I was nervous — maybe I needed a change.

Before I even went to Dante, I knew he was difficult. Friends had gone to his shop and never gone back because of his rudeness. He's lost many more customers than he's held on to, but I do have one friend who has been his customer for thirty years, so I knew a long relationship with him was possible, if rare. When I finally went to his salon, he wanted to know why I chose him, and who was my last hairdresser, and why did I leave him? Maybe I should have brought a written description of my hair history and a recommendation.

At this first appointment he laid down the ground rules:

1) Never be late.

2) I know more about your hair than you will ever know.

Of course over our almost twenty-year relationship, I was sometimes late due to construction on the road, snowstorms, car trouble. No lateness is excused — I was always punished for it. The punishment is swift and direct: I barely get a haircut; he goes through the motions but very little hair is removed, but the price is the same. When I arrived five minutes late for my last appointment, Dante was already on the phone calling my house to see where I was. In retaliation I guess, or maybe because I had proved unreliable, he asked me to come ten minutes earlier than my appointment time in the future, so I could wait for him rather than the other way around.

Since he obviously knows so much about hair, how could I ever presume to tell him what to do? Once in a great while, if I spoke in a soft, placating voice, I could request a minor alteration to my hair cut, to which he may or may not agree. Several months ago, I asked him to cut my hair a little shorter. He became impatient, then said irritably: "Of course I'll cut your hair shorter. It's summer, isn't it? Everyone gets a short cut."

A few years ago Dante complained about the way my hair looked when I came to the salon. I told him: "I'm here for a haircut. That's why my hair looks bad." He told me that my hair is a reflection on him (it's not like I was wearing a sign in my hair with his name on it) and that I was responsible for having good-looking hair at all times. I started ducking into the shop and going straight to the sink so that the assistant could wash my hair: that way Dante would first see my hair wet, and unstyled. He also told me that it was obvious that I didn't know how to blow dry my hair properly, and he would teach me. Once he even started, but then said it was impossible — I could never do it the way he did. He convinced me though to buy a new hair dryer, an item that would help me with my pitiful blow drying. He specially ordered the dryer, a huge affair in its own vinyl case, costing $100.

I nicknamed it the Pan Am because of its shape that vaguely resembled a jumbo jet, the loud noise it made when turned on and the vinyl carrying case that looked like something a stewardess would bring on a plane. This dryer had no effect on my hair styling whatsoever, mainly because it was too heavy and hard to manipulate.

During at least one third of my last appointment, Dante was not cutting my hair — he was either talking to the receptionist at the desk (not, incidentally, an attractive woman), whispering with his son at the back of the salon, or talking on the phone to various workmen who service his real estate holdings. Sitting in the chair, waiting for him to continue cutting my hair, I started to wonder if he would remember where he left off — I envisioned a lopsided cut. Meanwhile a different hair stylist stayed in one place, concentrated on cutting her client's hair and gave her what looked to me like a great haircut. I thought, "That's it, I'm switching. I can't take his rudeness and arrogance anymore — I must really be crazy to take his abuse. I've felt like a battered wife for too long, passive and too scared to act." Before I left I made an appointment with the lady hairdresser. I felt good — I was finished with him.

Several days later the salon called and left a message — there was a problem with my appointment. I didn't call back. The receptionist called two more times; I didn't return the calls. I imagined Dante stewing or at least confused about my appointment with someone else. Then I started to lose my nerve — maybe I should stay with him — I'm too old to switch. I called the salon and asked what was the problem? The receptionist mumbled something about another hairdresser, and I said "Of course my appointment is with Dante."

My friend gave me good advice. She said "keep your eye on the product. If you like the haircut, stay with him. He's not being rude to you, he is rude, period." In other words suck it up for the sake of looking good. Dante once told me I was vain because instead of going to a local hairdresser, I drove thirty minutes to his salon. I guess he was right.

A year later, I left Dante for good. I chose a hair salon that was run by women — no men on the premises. The haircut was cheaper, better, and the hairdresser was pleasanter. I even learned that Dante's wife gets her hair cut by my new stylist; she doesn't like the way her husband cuts her hair.

Afternoons at the Opera

In college I remember liking opera, somewhat. Truthfully, I am tone deaf — I can't distinguish between different notes and obviously can't sing. My father couldn't sing either and neither can one of my daughters, so I assume being tone deaf is hereditary. As a college student I would close my dorm room door, and put *Madame Butterfly* on the record player even though I didn't know anything about music.

When I lived in New York City, I went to The Metropolitan Opera a few times. I was a struggling high school teacher in Brooklyn and the opera was very expensive, as it still is. I could only afford the cheapest seats up in the balcony, so the singers looked like pygmies moving on stage but with chunky builds, burdened by heavy costumes. I couldn't understand a word since the operas were all sung in foreign languages and I never had any idea whatsoever of the plot. Once I fell asleep during a Mozart opera.

Fast forward to forty years later. I now live in Beverly, Massachusetts, approximately five hours from Lincoln Center and The Metropolitan Opera. A friend invited me to go to the multiplex in Revere to see a high definition movie of *La Traviata*, a live broadcast of a Met performance shown on a huge movie screen in stereo.

We arrived at the theater in plenty of time which turned out to be late. Almost every seat was filled, largely by Russians from Lynn and Revere who are such music lovers and culture hounds that they get to the theater two hours ahead of time, to get the best seats. The only seats left were in the front, so when I looked up, I could see the insides of the singers' mouths because the screen was so large. But I loved the show. I knew what was going on because there were subtitles on the screen, I could see everything, especially the tenor and soprano who were married to each other and practically making love on stage (they have since divorced). The opera singers were more like movie stars, beautiful, charismatic, shapely and immensely talented. Even with my bum ear I could appreciate the singing.

I thought I had it made — the Revere multiplex was my new Lincoln Center. I would get to a performance at least an hour early, so I could get a good seat. The performances are usually at 1 PM on Saturday. I know I can't sit through an opera without lunch so I sneak a sandwich, a piece of fruit and my water bottle into the theater ("No Food From Outside," the sign says). Unlike the food at Lincoln Center — wine, nuts, candy — the multiplex offers pizza, franks and a full bar, but I prefer a sandwich from home.

I even started to think that Revere was better than Lincoln Center. After all, it's less expensive, the seats are always good, I don't have to dress up, it's easy to get to and parking is free. However there is a drawback. Maybe because everyone gets to the movie theater an hour ahead of time, and eats in the theater, the atmosphere feels more like a movie theater (which it is) than an opera house. They even sell food inside the theater as well as in the lobby. There is some confusion as to whether this is a movie or an opera that I am seeing — it's both.

And maybe that is why I was ready to kill the five people sitting behind me at the last opera/movie I attended. They talked throughout the entire performance. Just as I was settling into a beautiful aria from the handsome tenor, the women would start what sounded like hissing behind me. When the women stopped, the men would start, talking as loudly as if they were drinking beer in a bar. Three times I turned around to ask them to be quiet — the men took that as a sign to talk louder. I enjoyed the opera, kind of, but the noisy fivesome ruined the mood and in opera mood is everything. Of course, I'm going back to Revere, but I know it's not exactly like going to the opera, it's more like attending a sporting event.

But I remember going to the opera in Italy: the opera house was a beautiful new art deco building in Florence. The members of the audience were glamorously dressed in the latest Italian fashion. The conductor and the director were world famous. Pasta was available during intermissions; the audience talked all during the performance and even cheered when a favorite aria was sung. Who needs The Met if Revere is more authentic?

Hotels

Since my daughter moved to New York City fifteen years ago, I have visited her about three times a year, always staying in a hotel near her two different tiny apartments. After approximately forty-five visits, all uptown on the West Side of Manhattan where she lives, I consider myself an expert on the hotels in this neighborhood which range from luxurious to places where no one should be caught dead (a body was found in one of the hotels).

The best hotel was the Lucerne, the first I stayed in, a tall, beautifully restored turn of the century place made of pink stucco with decorated cornices, the jewel of the neighborhood, located on the corner of Amsterdam Avenue and 79th Street. I had a contact at the hotel, remote but helpful, the sister of the wife of a friend's son, who was able to upgrade my room. As a result, I always stayed in a king suite which was larger than most New York City apartments. Though the kitchen was small (a typical NYC kitchen), it was modern with granite counter tops, up-to-date stainless steel appliances, and a marble breakfast bar. Furnishings in the living room were dark, heavy, hotel-style furniture — big chairs, a sofa covered in dark purple velour and out-sized lamps in peculiar places. The two ample-sized bedrooms each had a king-size bed with coordinated accessories — pillow shams, matching bed skirts, throw pillows, stripped comforters and high-end cotton sheets (no polyester here). I didn't want to leave after my three night reservation. I wanted to sell my house and move in, live right in the heart of the city, a few steps from all the excitement.

People do still live in the Lucerne, but not the movie stars who resided there in its heyday. In the thirties, my father, who worked his way through City College as a Western Union Telegraph messenger, delivered a message to Mae West at the hotel — she was half dressed. Cary Grant lived twenty blocks downtown in the Plaza on 59th Street. By the time I checked in to the Lucerne, in the early 1990's, the residents living there were, for lack of a better word, leftovers from a time when the hotels and surrounding neighborhood, beginning in the 1950's, had become run-down and dangerous. Homeless people lived on the street; the area became known as the heroin center of the city. The father of a friend had his suit stolen from the locked trunk of his car when he parked on the street while visiting his son. The once handsome three story brownstones, built around the turn of the century, were broken up into tiny apartments with the bathroom in the hallway. Elegant hotels like the Lucerne became brothels, flop houses and rooming houses for people who could only afford to live in one room apartments, mainly single people with nowhere else to go. Starting in the 1980's the neighborhood, like the rest of New York City, started to gentrify along with the old formerly elegant hotels. Because of rent control, the Lucerne, like other hotels in the neighborhood, was legally prevented from evicting residents from their apartments, so what developed was a quintessential New York City scenario — tourists staying in renovated hotels side by side with poor people who had lived in the hotel for many years but obviously not in renovated king-size suites.

As the hotels became nicer and nicer, they became, of course, more expensive, so as the neighborhood went up, my accommodations went down. After I couldn't even afford my "special deal" at the Lucerne, I stayed in a Quality Inn on 94th Street for many years. "The Dump" as I nicknamed the place, was reasonably priced because it was an exception to the renovation mania taking hold in the neighborhood; the Quality Inn was always in the process of renovation, but strangely never renovated. A sign on the elevator door read "WE ARE RENOVATING," but no improvements ever appeared — maybe the sign was an excuse for the elevator that was always breaking down. On the weekend that I helped my daughter buy a wedding dress, I found three cockroaches in my room — two in the bathtub, and one on the floor near my bed. My future son-in-law advised me to complain, not by saying that there were three roaches but instead numerous roaches, technically correct if not exact. I finally did get a refund but not before the desk clerk explained that the cockroaches were due to the renovations going on in the hotel.

One weekend while staying at "The Dump" I splurged for an opera ticket at the Met. In the early evening I was going up to my room to change when the small elevator in the lobby broke down suspending us between the basement and the first floor with the elevator door stuck open. Six of us were huddled together for forty-five minutes, trying to act adult and not panic. Because the door was open, I had a clear view down the shaft into the basement and could watch the machinations on the almost one hundred year-old elevator (as old as the hotel). After the hotel staff unsuccessfully fiddled with the machinery, an outside repairman was called. He arrived with a confident, determined air, like any hired gun, with a suitcase of tools, and was obviously familiar with the elevator because he didn't waste any time poking around, but got right to work and quickly fixed the problem. I made it to the opera on time, but not before a hotel employee blamed me for the broken elevator because I was the last one on, and obviously my weight was the tipping point. A long-time resident of the hotel took me aside, "Don't listen to him. The elevator is always breaking down." I began to use the freight elevator in the back lobby, a large rickety affair which didn't inspire much more confidence.

After several years of staying at "The Dump," the price of a room, unbelievably, went way up. Although almost seventy, I decided to try a youth hostel. The one I chose had a welcoming awning over the front door and was down the street from my daughter's new apartment on Riverside Drive. My German friends always stay in youth hostels when they travel, so I thought "How bad can this be?" After walking in under the attractive awning and through the misleadingly decent-looking front door, I reached the small front lobby. I was stunned — the place looked like an opium den (at least how I imagined one): people crowded in a small space, even in the hallways, lighting dim and hazy with a few bulbs scattered around. Instead of being bent over opium pipes, long-haired, glassy-eyed twenty-somethings were hunched over wi-fi connections, looking like they were communicating with the universe. No one moved, including the employee lounging at the front desk. A few broken-down sofas along with large velvet-like wall hangings were the only furnishings. Indecipherable music blared.

I wanted to leave immediately, even before I saw my room, but I knew I couldn't find another place at the last minute. The small elevator worked, a surprise after my years at "The Dump." The hallway reeked of pot. I had "splurged" (even here there were jacked-up New York City prices) for a single room with a private bath rather than a double that I would have to share with a stranger (man or woman) or even less appealing, a large room with six bunk beds, co-ed of course, and a large dormitory-style bathroom down the hallway. I scurried into my crowded, shabby little room and left only when I had to.

The last hotel, The Carter, located in Times Square was the worst, even worse than the youth hostel, but like so many peculiarities in New York City, it was next door to a fancy hotel with doormen and limos pulling in and out. The lobby in my hotel had a sign, "We no longer rent rooms by the hour." No room had a private bath. The bathroom turned out to be not a large, shared bath, but a small dirty room with exposed pipes, probably the original plumbing, down the hall, quite a distance from my room. I showered in my daughter's apartment. It was never clear how many guests used this bathroom, but there was a steady stream of people in and out.

Unfortunately, I stayed there during the New York City bed bug scare of a few years ago. The Carter was not cited on the NYC Hotel Bed Bug Site, but, unsurprisingly, "The Dump" was. I didn't trust the Bed Bug Site (could they check every room?) so I followed a friend's advice: bring a flashlight, take off the covers on the bed, (easy because of a thin blanket), run the flashlight along the edge of the mattress. Bed bugs are tiny and black — even though I didn't see any, I started to feel sorry for myself in this awful place; I was pushing old age, a school teacher, mother, with money in the bank — I didn't belong here even though I had chosen it. Maybe I'm cheap — I could have spent more money to stay in a nicer place, but I only sleep in the hotel; the rest of the time I spend with my daughter and her family. Plus there is a certain, call it, curiosity and guts factor — anyone can stay at a Marriot — but there is an "anthropological" interest in visiting out of the way places. The Carter though put an end to my exploring bargain hotels, but I did stop complaining. What about people who live in much worse conditions than the places I had been frequenting who did not have the choices I have? Was I a princess, like the princess and the pea in the fairytale, who was too delicate and spoiled for real life? I stayed (I didn't have a choice), but I enjoyed some of the cute young guys, half dressed, in the hallway on their way to our shared bathroom.

I'm glad I wasn't reading TripAdvisor when I stayed at The Carter because I would have discovered that the hotel was named the dirtiest hotel in America in 1996, 1998 and 1999 which included the time I stayed there. According to TripAdvisor, The Carter even had bugs that greeted guests in the lobby, in addition to a dead body found in one of the rooms. But the good news is that the hotel is now on the up-swing; thirty rooms on the fourth floor have been renovated with Ikea furniture and framed artwork bought from street vendors. And the bugs? No longer a problem because an exterminator comes through weekly with a spray gun.

But I lost my nerve. I've started crossing The George Washington Bridge to New Jersey where I can check into a Marriott, get a room with a private bath, clean shower, and even breakfast for a reasonable price. But it's not the same — there's nothing to explore in the burbs.

Family

NM

The playwright Henrik Ibsen's last play is *Ghosts*. Ibsen's ghosts don't wear white sheets and hide in the closet, but are family secrets kept hidden, yet too powerful to remain in the metaphorical closet forever. These embarrassing, painful secrets leak out in bits and pieces, at different times, and for that reason it is hard to know what's true and what's myth, or to understand the whole story.

NM was the ghost in my family. My relatives were loud, open with their feelings, revealing of themselves, telling us more than we wanted to know. The family all lived within a few city blocks of one another, in the Washington Heights neighborhood of New York City. Not NM. I had no idea where he lived; it could have been anywhere, even the moon. NM stands for Nathan Musher, my great grandfather — we never called him by his name, only his initials. The abbreviation only added to his mystery, a whole person, not a ghost would have a name. My great grandfather, my maternal grandmother's father, was in his early sixties when I was born and lived until his late eighties. He could have been a part of my life but I saw him only once, for less than an hour. He was a phantom really, someone always talked about, never seen — like a ghost he hovered over us. Where was he, what was he doing, how did he become rich (an important part of the legend)? I never visited him. No one in my family ever thought it was strange that we could have a close relative that we talked about and acknowledged was important but never saw.

In the twelve years I lived next door to my grandparents, NM visited only once. I remember tremendous anticipation regarding the visit. I felt as if we were getting ready for the King of England. My grandmother who was a strong, determined woman looked nervous and appeared to have almost shrunk in size (she was a tall person) when my parents and I arrived for the visit. For some reason I can only remember NM in the hallway of the apartment, a small, dark space that seemed to fit someone I had never seen before. He turned out to be a little man in a gray suit with a loud, self-important voice who was both threatening and disappointing: he was obviously in a hurry to leave.

My family was confused and upset after the visit — he was gone almost before he came, all our anticipation for what felt like so little in return. Later I learned that the reason NM agreed to come at all was because of money. My grandparents needed cash quickly for their faltering candy manufacturing business, and they hoped NM would give it to them; he did agree to give them something, but not the amount they were hoping for.

Even as a child, I knew a part of the story. When NM's young wife died, he disappeared leaving his three and five-year-old daughters, my grandmother and her sister, with their maternal grandmother. Their father never lived with his daughters again. But apart from these few facts, there were the rumors: NM had a second secret family who didn't know about his daughters from his first marriage: he lived faraway and had become very rich. According to the legend, NM secretly visited his two daughters and helped support them. I also heard that when NM died, my grandmother and her sister went to his funeral, but were seated in the back row of the chapel. They were not acknowledged by the "new" family consisting of sons, grandsons and maybe even great grandsons. How many of these rumors were true? Was there even a visit with NM that I was a part of almost sixty years ago?

Thanks to modern technology, a few months ago my brother was able to look up NM on the Internet, and discovered a few facts from archival newspaper articles. NM didn't exactly disappear at the time of his wife's death, but was in jail for forgery committed in New York City. He served a year and a half in Florida, and when he was released, he didn't return to New York City where his two daughters lived, but moved to Baltimore and started a new life. He was practiced at this — born in Russia, he somehow arrived in Palestine, then ended up in America. After jail, he changed one letter in his last name, from Musher to Mosher, married again, began a second family, had two sons and became rich in the olive oil business.

He began importing olive oil from Sicily, naming the oil "Pompeian" (he obviously didn't know Italian geography). The business became successful — I remember the green pyramid-shaped bottles of olive oil on supermarket shelves, not knowing, of course, that it was my great grandfather's business — eventually he sold the company to Kraft Foods for a huge undisclosed sum. He then recreated himself again — this time as an important Jewish philanthropist and supporter of Israel. He never publicly acknowledged his two daughters from his first marriage, and except for small amounts of money, never shared his great wealth with them. Pompeian Olive Oil is still on the shelves.

My grandmother and I were close, but she never revealed to me how hurt she was by her father's abandonment. She did marry a man who was the complete opposite of her father, someone not ambitious, but gentle, and very much in love with her. As a child, I never wondered why we called my great grandfather by his initials, unlike everyone else who had a name. After learning more of the story, I think it was my grandmother who started calling him NM for Nathan Musher or maybe even for No Man. I think it was too painful for her to call him father, or even Nathan, all she could manage were his initials.

At the heart of the mystery of NM, is how a Jewish immigrant who had been in jail, had no money or education and barely spoke English became wealthy in the Italian olive oil business. For me the story continues. I recently spoke to my Uncle Joe, my grandmother's son. He remembers when he was a child, seeing NM in my grandfather's candy factory in the Bronx mixing different kinds of oils, pouring the blended oil into bottles and labeling the bottles olive oil. I love this image of my immigrant great grandfather mixing up the oils, like a witch's brew, probably in the basement because who knows whether what he was doing was legal. I doubt it.

Hawk Family

Birds are part of our family psyche. Counting our birds plus our two daughters's birds, all wooden, hand painted shore birds, carved and painted by a family friend from New Jersey, we have eleven birds. Before I was married, I didn't know the difference between a pigeon and a seagull, but I quickly learned that Ed's family gave these special wooden birds as gifts for all occasions. We received, in the space of a few years, a tern, piping plover, pin-tail duck, and glossy ibis; when my daughter was married, the family gave her a beautiful, stylized pelican, her favorite bird, for an engagement present. The day after my father-in-law died, even before he was buried, the extended family divided up his twenty-five birds, the only valuables in his small apartment. We had more than enough birds, but since our two daughters hadn't yet arrived for the funeral, we represented our children in the division of the spoils. As we took turns, choosing birds, I secured a heron, a loon, a fly-catcher and one unidentified small bird for my offspring, just like any overly protective mother bird.

Given our interest in birds, it's not surprising that Ed alerted us to a small notice in the newspaper mentioning two red-tailed hawks building a nest on the ledge of the twelfth floor, outside the window of the office of the president of New York University. The University was so excited about these academic birds that they set up a webcam, directly on the nest. Violet, named for one of NYU's school colors, had laid three speckled eggs. When we looked at our computer screen, we saw a huge bird with brownish-black feathers and a large yellow, dangerous looking curved beak sitting on the eggs. Violet occasionally stood up to ruffle her feathers and stretch, but she stayed in the nest twenty-four hours a day (like Horton, the elephant, in the Dr. Seuss story). Once in a while, Violet would rotate the eggs or do a little light nest repair. The male hawk, Bobby, named for the Bobst Library where the president's office and the all-important ledge were located, arrived periodically with a bloody dead rat, squirrel or pigeon, a piece of which he'd pop into Violet's open beak. The bird experts weighed in on line to announce that the eggs, based on their estimate, would hatch between April 25th–30th.

I fell in love with Violet — a wonderful prenatal role model — and the unborn chicks; our increasing involvement with the hawks started to feel like a pregnancy in the family. Ed and I, our daughters, sons-in-law, three grandchildren and the science classes of our daughter spent a huge amount of time watching the nest online, waiting for an egg to hatch, a little like watching grass grow. April came and went — May came and still no chicks. Finally the experts announced that for some mysterious reason, the eggs were not viable: they would not hatch. We were all hugely disappointed — this felt like one of nature's dirty tricks, like a thunderstorm on July 4th. My daughter complained that she would have to face her young pupils with the sad news.

On May 7th, I came home late, and found a note from Ed: an egg had hatched. Violet had a chick who now felt like a new grandchild. When I spoke to my daughter the next day, Violet was feeding the chick an undefinable red morsel: baby hawks are meat eaters immediately. My young grandchildren were watching the screen in their apartment in uptown Manhattan, almost neighbors to the birds downtown. Our family felt like part of their family. But we were also hawk voyeurs, along with four thousand other viewers (according to the website): thanks to technology we could see what before was hidden. We could spy on their most private moments; fortunately they had bird brains and didn't know. We had all spent hours and hours watching Violet in the nest, often rushing into the house, and checking on her, before we took off our coats.

But for nature or, in this case humankind, difficulties are never far away. On Friday morning, the start of the Mother's Day Weekend, the chick was born, officially named Pip by New York University after a contest had been held to choose the best name, but by Saturday the news turned somber. A metal marking band on Violet's right leg, apparently put on incorrectly by a researcher, had moved up from her ankle to her shin: her leg was swollen to two to three times its normal size. There was a good chance her leg would fall off, and then she wouldn't be able to take care of the chick. Vi would almost certainly die, and so would the chick.

By Sunday the news was a little brighter. New York University called in a husband and wife team, hawk specialists but not veterinarians, from Long Island to try to save Violet and her chick (the other two eggs never hatched). The husband, using a harness, planned to go out a window, crawl along the twelve story ledge, capture Violet in a net, bring her back along the ledge and then into the building. The wife, using pliers and a wrench, would remove the band on the leg, give the bird an oral antibiotic (watch those talons) and pass her back to her husband who would make the return trip along the ledge to put Violet back on the nest. If this plan faltered, there was still a ray of hope. Should poor Violet not recover, Bobby might be able to take her place, not on the nest, but as a solo dad, hunting and feeding the chick. The plan was delayed a few days while the rescue team secured the proper harness for the dangerous maneuver with a huge terrified bird in a net. Phone calls went back and forth within our family, everyone nervously awaiting the results of Vi's ordeal.

The week dragged on — the special equipment was taking a long time to make; we worried that an injured mother would not be able to take care of our beloved chick. Five days after the hawk specialists' plan was first announced, the president of NYU called in the New York State Fish and Wildlife Association for a consultation. The special Health Care Team thought the ledge plan too risky and proposed putting bait (a dead rat? a dead squirrel?) on the roof of the building. Once Violet went for the bait, team members waiting on the roof would catch her in a net, do a quick repair on her leg, and place her back in the nest. On the scheduled day, I spent hours looking at Violet cuddled up to Pip, saw men walking along the roof, looking down at the nest but Vi did not take the bait — she never got off the nest. Occasionally, Bobby would drop by with a dead animal, Violet would chew some of the meat and feed Pip, beak to beak.

A new plan was put in place — the government and the specialists would do nothing. Violet was managing okay on her hurt leg, Pip was doing fine and even Bobby, though somewhat absent, was around occasionally. Violet was leaving Pip more, doing the hunting herself, but like devoted mothers everywhere, she always fed Pip first — he was getting bigger and hungrier. The hawks didn't need any human intervention.

After Ed and I came home from a vacation, we turned on the webcam and to our horror saw an empty nest. I thought Pip had fallen out of the nest and was certainly dead but a note on the screen reassured us nervous viewers that Pip was leaving the nest now, perching on the ledge, then coming back to the nest for meals. When I finally saw Pip, back in the nest, I couldn't believe how big and ugly he'd become in just two weeks: gone was the cute, cuddly chick and in his place was a gangly adolescent, all legs, big head and beak. Within a week, he had his flying feathers, but his distinctive red tail would come when he was a year old. I finally saw him practice flying on the ledge, right outside the nest. He stood perfectly still, then flapped his wings up and down, and made me afraid that he would fall. I worried about him, just the way I worry about my grandchildren when they look over a ledge in Riverside Park. But Pip knew what he was doing — he was getting ready to leave.

I felt sad about his upcoming departure and the soon-to-be-empty nest. But Violet and Bobby were in no way ambivalent about Pip's leaving — they helped him to go. They had been model parents, feeding him first, giving him the choicest pieces of meat, even mock fighting with him so he would be able to hunt on his own. But now that he was able to fly they were ready to push him out of the nest. The hawk parents brought a dead pigeon to the nest, then took the pigeon to the roof of a nearby building, making Pip fly to get his own food. I saw the young hawk gracefully fly from the nest and glide off in view of the camera. Pip's beautiful exit was the last I saw of him. An NYU security guard reported seeing the young bird in an alley between two buildings. His feathers weren't strong enough for him to fly up out of the alley but the clever bird was able to claw his way up the fire escapes to the roof.

Pip won't return to the nest — the nest is a nursery, not a home. Violet and Bobby will leave food for him in tree crevices for a month but then he is on his own. Luckily I have young grandchildren to love and worry over who won't be leaving the nest soon. Two days after Pip fledged, I visited the grandchildren and together we watched a replay of Pip flying off. My two-year-old grandson pointed to the screen, saying excitedly, "Hawk, Hawk." Maybe he'll be an ornithologist.

Country Life

I love cities though I haven't lived in one since the age of twelve. But I was born in New York City, surrounded by relatives on every block, and the excitement of city streets, and small, locally-owned stores. I am immediately at home in a city, any city, anywhere. I understand the vibe; I'm even more at home than in the suburb that I've lived in for forty years where I sometimes feel like I've just moved in.

Children stake out their own lives, of course, and like parents everywhere, I've learned to keep my opinions to myself. But I remember the sinking feeling I had the first time I drove up the small mountain in a remote part of western Massachusetts to visit my daughter and her boyfriend. They were living in Heath, a community of six hundred people, located in the foothills of the Berkshires. The drive up the road beginning at the bottom of the mountain to my daughter's house felt endless with woods on both sides of the road, a trip of about fifteen minutes. Finally I reached Heath Center which consists of a Community Center, a church, and a building that houses a small library, an even smaller post office, the office of the one policeman in town and a cluster of houses including the one my daughter was living in. Her boyfriend lived in an 18th century farmhouse attached to a small farm which included sheep, a llama and a big dog. I couldn't imagine how my daughter, born and raised in a lively suburb, close to a major city, would choose to live in such a remote place.

My daughter married her boyfriend and moved to the farm house permanently. I visited, stayed overnight, even in the winter though there was no heat in the upstairs bedrooms, but, fortunately, plenty of down comforters. A few years later their daughter Hazel was born who for the first few months of her life did not leave the vicinity of the wood-burning stove. When Hazel was six months old, Ed and I agreed that during my summer vacation from teaching (Ed had just retired), we would move to Heath to take care of Hazel while her parents worked. We rented a small cottage on a horse farm in Charlemont, a neighboring hill town, adjacent to Heath and equally remote. The cottage was filled with miscellaneous stuff (the owners used it as a dumping ground for what they didn't want in the main house) including the owner's deceased mother's many plants that I was told I was responsible for keeping alive.

Although Hazel was an easy baby to care for, she would not nap — she was later expelled from day care for refusing to sleep during nap time — so Ed and I always looked for ways to keep our wide-awake granddaughter amused. We started pushing her in the stroller up to the main farm where she could see the horses and goats. We were originally told on the web site that this was a "farm vacation" where we could help with various chores in the barns and with the animals. During our stay the owners never mentioned farm chores which was just as well because we had company every weekend from family and friends wanting to see "our farm."

Growing up in a city, I rarely saw animals except for stray cats and pigeons. My family took an occasional trip to the Bronx Zoo where the lone platypus, according to my father, the most unusual animal in the world, was the main attraction. No one in my citified family even had a pet. But as I started to feel loving and maternal caring for my granddaughter that summer, I realized that there wasn't only my granddaughter to be amazed about — I was surrounded by animals, many of them babies like her. Just as my granddaughter represented hope for the future so did the young animals living nearby. A foal was born on the farm and I saw it in all its wobbliness on the first day of life. But nothing was as exciting as the young Nubian goats. Nubians are large, gentle, sociable goats originally from Africa with noses that are described as "Roman" and long, floppy ears that hang down beyond their muzzle and form a bell shape. Nubians are nicknamed "Lop-eared Goat" or "Greyhound Goat." They are excellent dairy goats — the farmers in the area made goat cheese from their high-butterfat milk. The owner of the horse farm had five baby Nubians fed with a baby bottle who played when we visited. Down the road, the owner of a larger farm sold his gourmet goat cheese to high-end restaurants in Northampton and Amherst; he made ice cream from the milk of his Berkshire cows. The farmer allowed visitors to walk through his barns to see the Nubians, and to walk into his small field to see the Berkshire calves.

Another farm in the area, really a zoo, had what can only be described as an eclectic mix of animal life. Actually the owner called his place a fiber farm where he collected wool from various animals, then turned the wool into fiber for his weavings which he sold in a small store attached to his house. The main attraction was a twenty-year-old camel, but there were llamas, alpacas, peacocks and other assorted exotic birds. And there were the young — a baby camel, baby llamas, and baby peacocks.

Toward the end of the summer, my other two young grandchildren, Antonia and Nathan, arrived for a vacation. The highlight of the summer is the Heath Fair, an almost one hundred year-old agricultural fair held in the town's large fairgrounds. The whole town participates — for several years my daughter made her gourmet grilled cheese sandwiches (local cheddar, caramelized onions, green apple slices) to sell at the food booth. Along with the ox-pull, sheep shearing and square dancing is a petting zoo filled with baby animals. Along with my three grandchildren, miracles in their own right, and my connection to a future that at some point won't include me, were the animals with a future, young rabbits, sheep, alpacas, and donkeys.

I'm still a city girl but that summer enlarged my world. Now Ed and I carry binoculars on our walks so we'll be ready if an interesting bird flies by. I relate to my friends' dogs in a new way — I even look into their eyes. My favorite program on television is Nature. The other night a raccoon came up onto my back porch to look into the recycling bin. I felt honored by its presence and was sorry to see this large, beautifully colored animal depart.

City Life

The neighborhood of the upper reaches of the Upper West Side of Manhattan, just south of Columbia and Harlem, is almost an undiscovered neighborhood, if that is possible in New York City. Probably because of its proximity to Harlem with its reputation for drugs and violence, the area has not yet become overly gentrified. The neighborhood runs from Central Park West to the Hudson River, from about 90th to 110th Street. Tree-lined streets with beautifully restored brownstones worth millions of dollars are around the corner from a big city project. Youth hostels whose rooms stink of pot (I stayed in one) are on the same block as hotels charging three hundred dollars a night. Broadway, running down the middle, is a street bazaar where trendy French cafés are next to Korean groceries next to Jewish owned tiny hardware stores that look as if they've been there since biblical times.

Everywhere I look there are children, in strollers, double strollers, soccer uniforms, riding scooters. Maybe because this is not a particularly pricey area, compared to other neighborhoods in Manhattan, many young families live here. Since most mothers in the neighborhood work, almost everywhere I see a child, I see a nanny who has a different skin color or a big age discrepancy or some kind of cultural difference like dress or hair style?

My daughter and her husband, who live in the neighborhood, both work so their nanny Estella takes care of the children, Antonia three and Nathan one during the week. Estella, somewhat shy and quiet, in her early fifties, is from Guatemala. Unlike other families who sometimes have three different nannies in three years (a nanny might get sick, or sick and tired of the kid and the family, or the kid and the family don't like the nanny) Estella has been the only nanny for my grandchildren since Antonia was three months old.

I visited one afternoon when Estella was taking the kids to a Central Park playground for an ice cream party, so I went along. The party was in honor of Antonio, the best friend of Antonia, who, like Estella, is from Guatemala; he was adopted by a Jewish couple who are screen writers. There were about twenty kids at the party, saying good-bye to Antonio who was moving to Los Angeles for the summer while his parents worked on a new movie. Every kid had a nanny, but to underscore the importance of the occasion, there were three parents who had taken time off from work to help. The mother of Anika gave the party. Anika's mother is Indian married to an African American. Anika's mother and father along with Antonio's mother stood behind a table and dished out the ice cream.

Recently a new nanny arrived in the neighborhood, Griselda, Antonio's nanny. She'd only been in the neighborhood a few months, but immediately took center stage. A stylishly slim, attractively dressed woman who presided over the party like the "hostess with the mostest" despite three parents in attendance. She introduced herself to everyone, making sure they felt comfortable and had seconds on ice cream. She greeted me like an old friend, even though this was the first time we met, telling me that her husband had been a doctor in Mexico City and her daughter lived in Italy.

All the nannies were either Caribbean or Hispanic. Unlike the kids who played with one another, colorblind to their differences, the nannies separated themselves along ethnic lines, the Caribbean nannies sitting on one bench while the Hispanic nannies sat on a different bench on the other side of the playground. I never saw them speak to one another.

After the party we walked home, Estella speaking Spanish to my grandchildren while they answered in English. We passed white mothers pushing black children in strollers, and black women pushing white children. Color was all mixed up like a checker board, but no one seemed to notice. I loved it — I felt like a citizen of the world.

I miss the mix of people. I retired this year from teaching at a Community College in Lynn, a working class town north of Boston, where the students are from all over the globe. I love the worldly connection outward rather than the insularity I feel when I return home to my suburb. But many students from the college's other campus, located in the all-white suburb of Danvers, don't want to take classes in Lynn because they are afraid of the more diverse student body. They are more comfortable in the Danvers campus where they think they will fit in better. And that is almost certainly true — just look at the nannies in Central Park. No other city has the mix of people, but even in New York, nannies don't socialize with nannies who are different. Maybe that is why I'm still living in my white suburb, not in downtown Lynn.

Beaches

Since I've always loved cities, I was surprised to realize how much the beach and ocean have been a part of my life, even a metaphor for growing up and growing old. Jones Beach on Long Island was my introduction to sand, water and waves. Once a summer on a Sunday, my father would drive my mother, brother and me about fifty minutes to the beach. As my father was driving into the parking lot, he always made the same speech: "We should be eternally grateful to Robert Moses, Parks Commissioner of New York, for his vision of a large beach front park open to the public." That was the problem — the public was always there.

This was before beach chairs or umbrellas: we each carried only a towel taken from the bathroom (no fancy beach towels in those days) that we had to wedge between the towels of other beach-goers' because the public was always there; we had to make sure not to fling an arm or leg over the stranger on the neighboring towel. Although I could swim, I didn't go into the ocean on these excursions, probably because my parents, lifetime city dwellers, were afraid of the ocean but I remember baking in the heat. In spite of not swimming and sand so hot that my feet burned when I stood up, Jones Beach was my destination to celebrate the first time I drove a car after finally getting my license on my fifth attempt. Fifty years later, I can still remember the thrill of being behind the wheel, driving to the beach with a friend.

Marriage to Ed brought me to the Jersey Shore. Ed's family had a boat that took us to private beaches, a culture shock after Jones Beach. When the family wasn't on their boat, they were in Brigantine, a resort on the Atlantic Ocean, fifteen minutes from their home. The town of Brigantine is perfectly flat (remember this is New Jersey) including the white, sandy beach which had a rickety old-fashioned boardwalk with a scary haunted house that was eventually demolished and replaced with a casino. Brigantine is where I first went into the ocean and learned to dive under a wave and not get flattened, or to jump over one to avoid getting knocked down and, most exciting, to position myself with my back to an oncoming wave, and at the exact moment in the life of the wave, allow it to envelop me as I rode the wave gloriously to the shore.

Just by chance, I moved from New York City to Beverly, a town on Massachusetts Bay with no ocean waves but calm water and rocky beaches. We had family outings on the beach, and the kids took swimming and sailing lessons. As a teacher, I had summers off, my daughters were out of school and we spent every sunny day at the beach, One year, on the day school started, although it was September, the weather screamed beach, so after school, I packed up our gear and took the kids down the street to the beach. But it was almost fall, not summertime; I felt the pressure of work, the girls' minds were on their school friends — we couldn't recapture the feeling of those lazy, summer days.

After the kids grew up, Ed and I started spending almost every Sunday on the beach on Plum Island, a barrier island in the Atlantic, forty minutes from Beverly. Here the waves were powerful with a dangerous rip tide that people warned us about but we ignored — we were fearless in those days. The ocean was cold, never above the low fifties, but I spent hours in the water riding the waves. Once a wave was so powerful that I was slammed against the shore. The rough water went so far into my ear canal that I needed to see a doctor who, with a special tool, sucked the water out. One Labor Day Weekend, when Ed's brother and sister-in-law came for a visit, the weather was cold and rainy, but we spent every day of the three-day-weekend on Plum Island, the women huddled in raincoats and blankets while the men cast for bluefish from the shore.

Years later I returned to Brigantine for a family visit. The weather was hot and I ran straight into the water, not even bothering to put on suntan lotion. The surf was gentle, but suddenly, I was afraid of the ocean. I felt unsteady and knew I could get knocked down by waves I would have ignored when I was younger, but now I had poor balance and arthritic knees. I did get knocked down, and because of my weak knees I couldn't get up. The surf kept pulling me back into the deeper water which forced me to crawl on my hands and knees onto the sand. I stayed out of the ocean after that.

But then came the winter of 2014-2015 when Beverly had nine feet of snow and Ed broke his hip. In April we went to Jupiter, Florida, to recuperate. We had to choose between a condo close to the pool or to the beach. We chose the beach because as I told the condo manager, "We are beach people." Even though I hadn't been in the ocean for years, I still thought of myself as someone who, when faced with an ocean, would start riding the waves. The first morning we drove to the beach with all our gear — towels, umbrella, chairs, suntan lotion and lunch — we planned to spend a long time. The beach is pristine in Jupiter — no candy wrappers, beer cans, discarded towels, nothing but white sand and turquoise ocean. I went quickly into the water, expecting to swim ("we are beach people"), but then as gentle waves came in around my ankles, I was suddenly off balance, afraid of getting knocked down. I tried to get out of the water, but this time I couldn't — the surf kept pulling me back in. Finally, Ed, who uses a cane, walked to the water's edge, gave me a hand, and pulled me out of the ocean.

Meanwhile people were in the water, jumping over and under the waves, like I once did. Sitting in a beach chair watching them, I felt old — I knew the pleasure of the ocean was over for me. We left the beach sooner than we expected, lugged our stuff back to the condo and swam in the pool.

Friends

Visiting Alice

Alice and I met the first year I started teaching at a local community college in Massachusetts. From the beginning, I could see that she was different from the other teachers in the English Department; she never tried to impress people with her teaching credentials or literary sophistication. Her directness was almost scary. After knowing her only a short time, I felt like she knew all my defenses and pretensions, anything I was trying to hide without even knowing I was hiding it. I once described a fellow teacher as full of energy and high spirits, but Alice disagreed — she knew he was depressed because when he wasn't talking and the center of attention, he looked sad.

Although I assumed Alice was just a few years older, I have always thought of her as much older. She had the demeanor of someone who had lived a long time. Even in her fifties, when we met, her hair was gray, never dyed. Alice did not appear to come from any particular place although she was born in Gloucester, Massachusetts, not far from Essex where she lived. She was not especially literary although she had her favorite authors, Saul Bellow for one, a Jewish writer from New York City whose background and experiences could not have been more different than hers. She never spoke of her family (she was childless and divorced) except for one cousin who lived nearby. What was the source of her personal power felt by me and other people? Maybe it was her outspokenness or honesty or intelligence, a refusal to be anyone but herself.

But part of her power, I believe, was a tragedy she somehow managed to survive. For years I had heard whispers that something awful had happened to her. Alice was too private, too self-contained for me to ask about the rumors. Finally a colleague told me that her young daughter had died; her husband, suspected of killing the child, yet not charged was committed to a mental hospital. I couldn't reconcile this event with the woman I knew — nor at first could I believe the story, the event was too terrible. Alice gave the impression of not having a past, and I couldn't picture her as someone's mother or wife. When I met her, I didn't see any signs of the tragedy in her life. Alice lived alone in a small antique house she had recently bought: she had a full life, tickets to The Boston Symphony, travel, friends. When I knew her better, I began to think that maybe the pain of her child's death, and her subsequent divorce had become so much a part of her that she had become a different person, someone whose past was hidden, buried deep inside.

After a couple of years at the college, we became friends. Alice acted as if I knew what had happened, even though she never told me. Only twice did we talk about the tragedy. Once while we waited for a meeting to start, she described running into her ex-husband who had recently been released from a mental institution. Another time she told me about the snowy night her daughter died, and how she had run out of the house to find help.

What helped Alice go on with her life after the death of her daughter was her friendship with Clara, a German Jewish refugee who had also suffered a tragedy early in her life. When Clara was nine, she and her parents were put in a concentration camp in Germany. All three family members survived the war because as Clara told me, "We were in the model camp, Theresienstadt, the place the Swiss Red Cross visited and then declared that prisoners were treated well." After the war the family moved to Texas where Clara became a college math teacher and the editor of a well-known book on the history of math. Clara and Alice met at a girl's school in Texas where they were both teaching and became life-long friends. Tragedies in their lives deepened their friendship, and they became the most important people in each other's lives.

After fifteen years of teaching with Alice at the community college, the administration forced her to retire. She had chronic pain in her shoulder, two operations on her right rotator cuff, and was missing many days of teaching. After she left, the college felt empty without her. I needed Alice as a friend and ally, my barometer to test the sometimes murky atmosphere of the place.

After her retirement, Alice disappeared from my life — it was as if she wanted to erase all aspects of her teaching life that had meant so much to her. She didn't return phone calls or cards. Maybe ten years after her retirement, she sent me a self-published mystery that she and a friend had written about a crime that took place within a tour group visiting Egypt. I sent a card thanking her for the book, telling her how much I liked it and suggesting we get together. No reply. Occasionally I would drive by her house on the way to somewhere else, see her car and think, *well, she's still alive.*

Over a year ago, I received a phone call from Alice who acted as if it were the most natural thing in the world that we would be talking together as friends after a twenty-year break. Her health wasn't good — twenty years earlier she had been diagnosed with Parkinson's Disease but had kept it a secret from everyone but close friends. Clara had been living with her for many years because she needed help — they had been talking about me — could I come for coffee?

I was surprised to hear from her, pleased that she wanted to see me, glad to hear that she was still alive, and looked forward to seeing Clara after all these years. When I arrived at her small house, Alice was sitting in a wheelchair, at the dining room table. Her Parkinson's was severe: she couldn't walk, could barely speak or eat. The room was dark and crammed with stuff: lamps, knickknacks, books, pictures. Alice couldn't do housekeeping, and Clara, a math genius, was not interested in housework or in cooking, according to her friend. Clara was in and out of the kitchen, getting iced tea for Alice and me, although the weather was cold.

I wondered how these two women could keep going under such trying circumstances? Because of Alice's illness, their lives were almost completely confined to the small, over-stuffed rooms of Alice's house. But after my shock at seeing her so changed, I realized she was the same person I had known twenty years before. She made her usual barbed comments about our fellow faculty members, laughed at her old office mates, and told me she was glad I brought just a few pictures of my grandchildren, rather than foisting hundreds on her; she had clearly kept her edge. Alice even complained about Clara when she wasn't in the room: "Clara thinks she's a good cook but she isn't," but it was obvious that the two women were devoted to each other. When Clara finally sat down, the three of us talked for a long time — as if twenty years had not gone by since our last conversation. These two old women who had suffered so much somehow were able to put the past behind them and engage in life. We talked about books, music, history, food, gossip, movies, TV. Shirley even confessed she was eighty-eight; I had assumed she was much younger.

For a year and a half I visited them at their house. The visits were always in the afternoon — it took Alice that long to get ready for visitors (she dressed well, her hair done attractively). I heard stories about their childhoods. Once Clara talked about a well-known German Jewish actor her family knew who was killed by the Nazis in Theresienstadt while she was there. The actor thought he would be protected if he pretended to be sick, but that only gave the camp guards an excuse to kill him and his wife. On my next visit we watched the actor in the German movie "The Blue Angel" starring Marlene Dietrich. Alice commented that Dietrich looked heavier than she remembered. Once we watched a program on Aaron Copeland, a favorite of theirs, and both women were big fans of Robert Caro's latest book on Lyndon Johnson.

Although we were a threesome, sometimes just Alice and I talked, while Clara made tea and Alice complained about how slow and absent-minded she was. Toward the end of the visit, Alice would get tired and nod off and then Clara and I would talk. She told me about her Jewish father and Christian mother and how her mother refused to abandon her father to the Nazis.

On my last visit we ate fried clams. Spring had finally arrived after a long, cold winter, and the ladies wanted to eat the local speciality. Their favorite clam shack in Essex, Farnams, had just opened, and both women were looking forward to eating the first clams of the season. Alice wanted to go in the car to pick up the clams, but Clara wanted to leave her behind with me. These two elderly women who had been through so much started arguing — neither one willing to give in. Finally Clara strapped Alice in the wheelchair so she wouldn't fall out and left us in the house together. I realized this was the first time I had been alone with her since I had started visiting. We started talking openly, about ourselves, the people we felt close to and how even when you love someone, you can get angry at them. Without Clara as a buffer, it was just Alice and me, reminiscent of when we became friends, almost forty years ago. I had a chance to really look at Alice that afternoon, and I could see that she was dying, and she knew it.

Clara returned with fried clams, onion rings, French fries and cans of Moxie (a special soda, brown-colored and overly sweet that Alice liked). Alice couldn't hold a fork, so we ate with our fingers. Eating this summery food, like a picnic, with a friend who was so sick, I was honored that they would share this meal with me. Looking back, this dinner was like the last dinner I had with my father before he died, unforgettably sad but deeply moving. At these dinners, both my father and Alice were the way they always were, remarkably alive and responsive but keenly aware that they were close to death.

Passover and Easter coincided that spring. Alice sent me a plant of beautiful white lilys, definitely more Christian than Jewish, but the card said, "Happy Holidays." She then left her standard message on my answering machine, "Alice Rogers here." Her voice was always recognizable but her speech was hard to understand. I never had the chance to thank her for the plant. When I called back, Clara told me she wasn't doing well, but Alice would call me in a day or two. She never called, although I left messages on her voice mail. Two weeks later Clara called to tell me that Alice had died.

Before Alice died, I didn't understand why she telephoned me after a twenty year absence. But looking back on her phone call, I believe Alice knew she was dying and had decided to see old friends before it was too late. She and Clara continued to go out to lunch. Clara read books aloud to Alice in the evening; they tried to live as fully as possible, the way they always had. On my last visit, when the two of us were alone, Alice looked at me, and her face conveyed, without having to say anything, that she knew her life was over. After she died, Clara told me that she realized that not only did Alice understand other people, but she understood herself, and she accepted her death.

Heath

His name suggested the outdoors, something vaguely wild, and always made me think of the handsome Australian actor Heath Ledger who died of a drug over-dose. Heath looked nothing like the actor. He was slight, weighing only about one hundred and thirty pounds, short, maybe five foot four, in his early forties, handsome, with a plain, open face and straight light brown hair down to his shoulders. I suspected he changed his name to Heath as part of his drive to recreate himself when he finally landed a full-time job teaching at the community college in Massachusetts where I taught. He had spent years as an adjunct teaching part-time at different colleges. Heath was from Virginia, home of great Southern cooking, and, according to him, his whole family was fat. He told me he was once fat, like the rest of his relatives, but that he lost sixty pounds the year before he came north. He had never lived outside of the south or near water before he moved to Massachusetts. In addition to a new place to live and a new job, Heath had a new wife who was finishing up her job in Virginia, and she was pregnant.

When I retired from full-time teaching, Heath was hired to take my place: the year he came I taught part-time, two days a week. We shared an office with two other faculty members. Heath worked at a small table, I worked at my desk, our shoulders practically touched. I am old enough to be his mother; my daughter is thirty eight, close to his age, but Heath never treated me like an older woman, who only taught part-time, and was thus irrelevant. Instead, he viewed me as a colleague with many years of teaching experience that counted for something. He was a southerner with a courteous, deferential manner who spoke with a slight southern drawl and addressed all women, except the young, as "ma'am." I liked talking to him and looked forward to seeing him in the office. If I had not retired, Heath would not have been at the college, so I felt a certain responsibility toward him; as my replacement, I wanted him to succeed.

Heath was not the typical college English teacher. Maybe because he had lost so much weight and was determined to stay thin, his eating habits were strange: he only ate uncooked food. When colleagues went out to lunch, Heath would drink tea, a special tea from the mountains of Peru that he had recently visited. Lunch for him was never in the faculty dining room, but at his table in the office where he ate chopped nuts, fruit, and grated vegetables that he prepared at home. He lived alone because his wife was teaching at the University of Virginia where her subjects were psychology and sexual compatibility. Heath told me that a large part of her Ph. D. research consisted of watching pornographic movies. According to Heath, she fell in love with him because he didn't laugh at her research.

Soon after the beginning of the semester, Heath developed a close friendship with another faculty member in the English Department, someone who had been at the college a few years longer. Both men were about the same age, new to the area and newly married but were otherwise like Mutt and Jeff. In contrast to Heath's smallness and somewhat reserved manner, Rob was big and beefy-looking with a booming voice and a loud personality. When I first met Rob, he reminded me of a California surfer who had accidently washed up on the coast of Massachusetts: like a surfer he had long blond hair, wore brightly colored Hawaiian shirts, even in the winter, and flirted constantly with students and young faculty members.

What drew the two of them together, I think, was that Heath was trying on a new self to go with his new job, new locale, and new marriage and Rob became his role model. The big guy and the little guy turned into a male buddy movie, American style. Rob was even from California and actually a surfer (he started a Surfing Club at the college). He taught Heath to surf in Gloucester and Plum Island, they climbed Mount Washington and rode motorcycles like their hero, Jack Kerouac. During the semester Heath traveled to Peru and brought back special tea for Rob which they shared with me in the office. The two of them found an apartment for Heath near the coast in East Gloucester and Rob drove his truck to Virginia to help Heath move his furniture up to Massachusetts.

But by the middle of the year, Heath was no longer living alone and hanging out with the guys in the English Department because his wife had joined him in December after her teaching semester ended in Virginia. She was not how I imagined Heath's wife — I had pictured someone small and quiet like him. Instead, she was a big woman, loud, dominating, attractive and nine months pregnant. She towered and talked over him, sometimes belittling him. Their baby was born a few weeks after she arrived. One day in the office Rob confided that he didn't think he could be friendly with Heath and his wife because he didn't like Heath's wife. She was too strange for him. He was right, she was strange. She was a sex therapist who refused to have anything to do with doctors or hospitals. Rob and his wife were upset that she refused to have the baby in a hospital, only at home, even though she was diabetic.

I knew Heath's life would be different once he was living with his wife and baby, but I wasn't prepared for the complete change: the Heath I knew, even briefly, started to melt away. Instead of the gracious, engaged person I had become friendly with, he grew quiet and withdrawn. He looked more and more harried and started to have run-ins with students that became serious enough to involve the dean. His conversations in the office became more negative, especially about the college. Details from Heath's past that he shared with me seemed at odds with the man I knew. I learned he had a seven-year-old daughter from a previous unmarried relationship. Although he was in his early forties, he'd never had a full-time job before coming to the college. He had never done anything athletic until this year with Rob because he'd always been too heavy. Now his thinness worked against him — he looked like he was shrinking into himself. Once in the office, he told me that what he really wanted was not to work, but to stay home with his wife and baby.

Meanwhile, Rob was acting as his unofficial real estate agent, looking for a house for Heath and his wife to buy, maybe even down the street from Rob. We talked in the office about the possible choices, and Heath and his wife even bid on, but lost a house. Suddenly the house hunting stopped, Rob was no longer on the computer looking at real estate, and the office was eerily quiet. Finally, Heath told me, "We're moving back to Virginia.

I'm taking a year's leave of absence. I want to be closer to my mother, who is a widow." I was amazed — he had only been at the college a year. He added, "I know it's hard to give up a tenure-track position."

The spring semester ended with lunch and a workshop. Heath sat across from me, but kept his head down and didn't talk to anyone. When the workshop ended, he left quickly, without saying good-by. He never returned to the college, and no one, including Rob, has heard from him since.

The Salvation Army

In the early seventies, the Port Authority Bus Terminal in New York City was gruesome, a place to avoid, if possible: peeling paint, broken fixtures, the stink of cheap food, homeless people sitting on the floor, in every available spot, surrounded by their pitiful possessions. Ed and I were either arriving or departing, rushing as usual, when we came upon a large man, face down, stretched out on the floor, blocking our way. I said, "We have to step over him" which I did, one leg at a time. Ed hesitated, "Maybe he's dead."

"I doubt it," I said rushing ahead, "I'm sure he's drunk." I never knew whether he was dead or drunk because Ed stepped over him and neither of us looked back. But I couldn't forget him. Even now more than forty years later, I can see him lying there, the two of us stepping over him, not even bothering to look for help, treating a man like a bag of garbage.

But then I needed help, and was lucky to receive it, from an unexpected source, a homeless man. I was in the hospital for a complicated gall bladder operation, alone in a dreary room, cut off from my family and friends. One night about nine I heard a commotion in the hallway. When I opened my door, I saw two policemen holding a stretcher with a disheveled, slight, roughly thirty-year-old man sitting cross-legged, holding his belongings — tattered shirts, old bedding, underwear. The man was yelling, "I don't want to be here. Leave me alone. Leave me alone." The police ignored him, quickly escorted him into a room a few doors down from mine, and left him there.

Two days later, I met him in a common room in the hospital. He was no longer shouting, but was friendly, wanted to talk, and was ready to explain how he had become a hospital patient. I was lonely and willing to listen. Because he was homeless, he lived off and on in a Salvation Army Shelter, but he had become a nuisance, yelling at the other residents and getting into fights because he drank too much. The police had been called many times, but finally they became fed up and brought him to the hospital to dry out.

To the surprise of the hospital staff and patients who had witnessed his boisterous entry into the ward, he became a model citizen. Of course he couldn't drink in the hospital, but more than that, he felt cared for — he no longer had to fend for himself. The hospital provided him with his own room, clean sheets, meals. He had become an ordinary person, not someone who lived on the street or in a shelter.

I liked him and I wanted company. We started to hang out together: unlikely companions, a homeless man and a middle class woman from the suburbs. He was nothing like the man yelling on the stretcher, but gentle, a good listener, smart and knowledgeable about life. And in the hospital we were the same, just patients. I was there outside my life and what defined me: husband, children, job. For now he was just a young man in the hospital.

We talked about the other patients, nurses, doctors, what went on in the hospital. He was sad about the way his life was turning out, and he would say over and over, "I could be like you. I wasn't born this way." But we only talked about the present, not the past: our friendship was in the now. We had found ourselves together, unlikely mates, but we were able to comfort one another. I never learned the circumstances of his life that led to his homelessness.

After a few days, the nurses started talking about sending him back to the shelter. He became angry, started yelling, threw his hands in the air, refused to go. The next day two policemen came and took him away, not on a stretcher this time, but holding him firmly under his arms while he clutched his meager belongings. Before the police took hold of him, we gave each other a long hug in the hallway while a nurse looked on in disbelief at the odd couple: she didn't know him; to her he was just a homeless man, making a fuss about leaving. She couldn't understand why I would miss him.

Unlikely Friends

About fifteen years ago I spent a month in Perugia, Italy at the University, trying to learn to speak Italian. I have always wanted to speak another language, to try to enter into another culture, to be someone else. Italian seemed like a good choice. I had visited Italy many times, loved the country, the people, the food and the history. On these visits, I tried to pass for Italian, wore long, flowing dresses, tried to act freer and felt more womanly than I did in the States. So why not take my love for all things Italian one step further, and study the language so I could really enter into the culture?

I rented an apartment for a month in Perugia and enrolled in a language program. In my class was a nun around forty from Korea. We sat next to one another and became friends although she was very serious and always studying, unlike me. It was an unlikely friendship, a nun from Korea and a Jewish school teacher from Massachusetts. She was slight, seemed younger than forty but it was hard to tell because her body and face were overwhelmed by the heavy cloth of her gray habit and stiff wimple. Kim Chung's Catholic order had sent her to Italy to learn Italian; after three months she would move to Rome to work with the poor.

We stayed after class to help each other with Italian. We met for lunch in the town center and tried to speak Italian to the waiters and each other, although she complained that she didn't have extra money for luxuries like eating out. Once I saw her buying underwear in an Italian lingerie store — she looked embarrassed to be seen in such a fancy store.

I envied her in a way. I had to leave in a month, barely speaking the language, while she stayed on for two more months. I knew she was on her way to becoming fluent in the language, and would soon move to Rome and become completely immersed in the culture. She would belong to a different place while I would have had just a taste and soon return to my former life. I think of her sometimes, moving easily in Rome, having a new self, part of Italian life. I wonder if I could have done what she did. The funny thing is she didn't really like Italy. She complained about the weather, that the restaurants were windowless and in basements. She missed Brazil where she had been before.

The Art of Losing

A few weeks ago I lost my address book, the entire record of my social world. I realize address books are going the way of the dinosaurs — why write down an address when you can type it into a device? But I grew up in a world without computers: organizing the addresses and telephone numbers of the important people in my life, in one place, struck me as the height of organization. I owned my first book in my early twenties. Now seventy, I've owned five different books, approximately a different book for each decade of my life.

I had owned this latest book for at least ten years, because I remember carefully transferring names from my previous one while my father watched; he was the model for carefully kept records, and he died more than ten years ago. Now the book was not in good shape: the cloth cover, with a Biblical theme was torn, pages were loosened. I knew I nneded a replacement, but it was a daunting task, transferring a lifetime of connections into a new book.

I used to read my address book to review the history of my life. My daughters in their twenties and thirties moved around. Different addresses and phone numbers were carefully recorded and crossed out when they moved to a new place. One daughter went to college and graduate school in the mid-west, lived in Japan, later moved to New York City for a first job and her own apartment, then moved again. Another daughter attended college on the west coast, worked at an outdoor school in Maryland, moved to New Hampshire for a master's degree, to Vermont for a teaching job and back to Massachusetts where she now teaches.

My friend Bill's name was recorded; he died of cancer several years ago. Seeing his address and telephone number reminded me of how much I loved and missed him. My father's trajectory at the end of his life was recorded: first his Long Island address, next the move to Florida, finally the Beverly address where he moved to be close to me and Ed.

Before my father died, he gave me his address book, the rich record of his long and full life. I had the task of calling my father's friends and family to tell them of his death. Because everyone was listed in his book, calling was easy. I've kept his book because, to me, it's a record of his life — I'm heartened by reading it.

How did I lose my address book? I was rushing. Although I knew it was foolish to take it out of the house, I did. I needed my sister-in-law's address in Arizona to mail her a Christmas present. After the post office, I walked to the supermarket with the book under my arm. The last I saw of it was as I went through the checkout line; it was in the child's seat of the supermarket carriage. I went back a few hours later when I realized it was gone. No one in the grocery store had seen any sign of it — the book had vanished.

I felt naked without my address book. I had no record of my life: it was as though friends and family had disappeared. Even my daughters' peripatetic lives were lost to me. A few days later I searched for a replacement. I found only one in the different stores where I looked — obviously people are not using address books anymore. Names, addresses, phone numbers are all stored electronically. There are no more cross outs, just deletions. If a friend dies, it's easy to erase him from your iPhone.

My new book is glaringly white, a loose-leaf, with a sticker on the inside back cover giving a phone number if I want to order more pages. Will this company still be in business should I ever need new pages? I doubt it. I started to reconstruct my new book, address by address. Luckily it was two weeks before Christmas, so many return addresses were on cards sent to me. I made a few phone calls to get more addresses — I even found addresses from my email.

I began to like my new book. My life seemed more orderly. Each entry was carefully recorded with a lot of white space on the page: No cross-outs, no blurred ink, no torn pages, no painful names of friends I don't see anymore. There is a feeling of lightness, of going forward, a fresh beginning. I would have held on to my old book if I hadn't lost it, but I can see the benefit of letting go, starting over on a clean page. Besides, I still have my father's address book. When I first lost my book, I kept thinking of the first lines of Elizabeth Bishop's poem, "One Art."

> *The art of losing isn't hard to master*
> *So many things seem filled with the intent*
> *To be lost that their loss is no disaster*

Acknowledgements

Thank you to the Writing Group at the Beverly Senior Center whose members liked my early attempts to put my thoughts on paper and who encouraged me to keep going. The Senior Center was where I met Liz Moon. For more than four years, Liz and I met every two weeks at Panera to exchange our writing. Liz's editorial skills were a huge help to me. Liz made me feel like a writer, and I have no doubt that I wouldn't have completed this project without her support and enthusiasm for my essays. I met Peter Wilder and my late friend Donna Nutile at a *T'ai Chi* class in Topsfield. After class, the three of us met at a coffee shop, read our essays aloud and critiqued one another's writing; sharing my essays with them gave me the confidence to continue writing. Thank you to Marcus Alonso, my editor, who chose the cover and has done a terrific job in editing the manuscript.

Finally a big thanks to Ed who shared many of the experiences in this book with me and provided me with details I had forgotten. Ed was my first reader and editor for every essay, and in more than fifty years of marriage, he has never confessed to tiring of my stories.

Made in the USA
Middletown, DE
28 February 2016